W9-BVM-014

THE CHRISTMAS STORY

Tommy NELSON

Thomas Nelson, Inc.

Nashville

Published in Nashville, Tennessee, by Tommy Nelson™, a division of Thomas Nelson, Inc.

Originally published in 1993 by Thomas Nelson Publishers, Nashville, Tennessee.
Copyright © 1993 Bluewood Books

**Story retold by Bill Yenne
and Timothy Jacobs**

Edited by Lynne Piade. Art and design direction by Bill Yenne. Illustrated by Pete Avdoulos, Mark Busacca, Emi Fukawa, Victor Lee, Wendy K. Lee, Douglas Scott, Peggy Smith, Alexandr Stolin, Vadim Vahrameev, Hanako Wakiyama, Nelson Wang and Bill Yenne.

Produced by
Bluewood Books (A Division of The Siyeh Group, Inc.)
P.O. Box 689, San Mateo, CA 94401

The Christmas Story.
    p.   cm.—(Children's Bible Classics)
    Summary: Simple text describes the birth of Jesus on the first Christmas and recounts who came to see him.
    ISBN 0-8407-4916-3 (TR)
    ISBN 0-8407-4912-0 (MM)
    1. Jesus Christ—Nativity—Juvenile literature.
2. Bible stories, English—O.T. Gospels. [1. Jesus Christ—Nativity. 2. Bible Stories—N.T. 3. Christmas]
I. Thomas Nelson Publishers. II. Series.
BT315.2.F57   1993
232'.92—dc20   93-24835
                                                              CIP
                                                               AC

Printed in Mexico
97 98 99 00 01 02 03 RRD 9 8 7 6 5 4 3 2 1

THE CHRISTMAS STORY

A very long time ago, a young woman named Mary lived in the small town of Nazareth. She was getting ready to marry a young carpenter named Joseph. Mary and Joseph were both very good people.

One day God sent the angel Gabriel to give
Mary an important message. "Don't be afraid,"
Gabriel said, "you are truly blessed."

Gabriel told Mary that she was going to be the mother of a special baby who would be called Jesus, and He would be the Son of God. Mary was surprised, but she believed the angel and trusted God.

Soon after Gabriel's visit, Mary
went to see her relative Elizabeth.
The Spirit of the Lord filled
Elizabeth and she was happy. She
knew that Mary would be the mother
of God's son.

Joseph loved Mary very much, but at first he did not understand that Mary was going to have a baby by God's Holy Spirit. Then, one night while he was asleep, he had a wonderful dream. The angel Gabriel told Joseph that Mary's baby would be the Son of God, and that they should go ahead with their plans to marry.

Joseph and Mary were happy that they had been chosen by God to raise Jesus. They knew He would be the Savior of the world. But when it was time for Jesus to be born, they were told they had to go to Bethlehem.

Mary and Joseph didn't want to go to Bethlehem just before the baby was born but they didn't have a choice. The Roman government ruled the land, and they wanted to count all the people who lived there.

Finally Mary and Joseph arrived in Bethlehem. The city was crowded with people who had come to be counted, so they couldn't find a place to stay.

They looked everywhere, but none of the inns had any room for them. Then, a kind innkeeper let them stay in the stable next to his inn.

It was here, where the animals slept, in the stable, that Jesus Christ was born.

The same night, on a hillside just outside of Bethlehem, some shepherds were guarding their sheep. Suddenly, they saw an angel before them. The brightness of God's glory shone around them.

"Don't be afraid," the angel said. "I have good news for you. This very day in Bethlehem, a Savior was born for you. He is Christ the Lord. You may see Him there."

"He is a newborn baby, wrapped in soft clothes, and lying in a manger."

The shepherds, who loved God, hurried to Bethlehem. They found Mary and Joseph, and the baby Jesus, just as the angel had said.

Far away in a land to the east, there lived some wise men. One night they saw a strange new star in the sky. They had read that the Son of God would be born on Earth someday, but nobody knew when. When they saw this new star, they were sure that it was a sign from God that the time was very near.

The wise men set out to follow the star and find the newborn king.

When they reached Jerusalem, they went to King Herod. They were sure he would know where the new king would be born. Herod didn't know anything about the birth of a new king. But he knew the stories the old men told about a Son of God, and he was jealous. He wanted to be the only King around.

Herod told the wise men to look for the new king in Bethlehem. "Go and search there carefully for this little child. When you have found Him, please come and tell me, so that I, too, can go worship Him."

Herod was lying so he could find out where the baby was and kill him.

The wise men followed the star until it stopped right over the place where Jesus was.

The wise men knew that this baby was the Son of God, and they worshipped Him. They gave Him gifts of gold and precious incense, called frankincense and sweet-smelling myrrh.

God warned the wise men in a dream that King Herod was angry and jealous. They knew he might hurt the baby Jesus, so they never told him where the child was.

God protected Jesus and His parents from Herod.
As the shepherds and wise men knew, the baby they had
seen would grow up to be the great king and Savior of
the world.

Joseph and Mary eventually returned to their home in Nazareth, where Jesus would grow into a man. Then Jesus would perform wonders and miracles such as the world had never seen.

This is the story of the very first Christmas. Today people all over the world celebrate the birth of that little baby so long ago.